T0345797

A queer and queered series of love poems, *risk :: nonchalance* carries forward questions about love, art, and philosophical questioning. Contemplative, roaming, loving, wondering, the poems offer pathways even as it offers contradictions, "a map that never stops."

hoa nguyen, *author of VIOLET ENERGY INGOTS*
judge of the Omnidawn Poetry Chapbook Prize

risk :: nonchalance

ALSO BY laura neuman

Stop the Ocean, Stockport Flats (2014)
The Busy Life, Gazing Grain (2012)

risk::nonchalance

laura neuman

OMNIDAWN PUBLISHING
OAKLAND, CALIFORNIA
2017

Cover image: *The Repressed / The Return of the Repressed* by Emmy Bright, silkscreen and marker on paper.

Text set in Century Gothic and Garamond 3 LT Std

Cover and Interior Design by Sharon Zetter

Offset printed in the United States
by Edwards Brothers Malloy, Ann Arbor, Michigan
On 55# Glatfelter B18 Antique
Acid Free Archival Quality Recycled Paper

Library of Congress Cataloging-in-Publication Data

Names: Neuman, Laura, 1980- author.
Title: Risk: nonchalance / Laura Neuman.
Description: Oakland, California : Omnidawn Publishing, 2017.
Identifiers: LCCN 2017022796 | ISBN 9781632430465 (paperback : alk. paper)
Classification: LCC PS3614.E5528 A6 2017 | DDC 811/.6--dc23
LC record available at https://lccn.loc.gov/2017022796

Published by Omnidawn Publishing, Oakland, California
www.omnidawn.com   (510) 237-5472   (800) 792-4957
10 9 8 7 6 5 4 3 2 1
ISBN: 978-1-63243-046-5

I prefer 'you' in the plural.

john ashbery

sincerity: this determination
to commit the fault.

rob halpern

For Eero

::

::

How big the room is really matters for you, marysia.

Tracking shot ethics:
I'm fucked, marysia.

I write because that thought seemed to arrive as a writing action.

I believed you about the scissors I believe you now.

How does writing become a poem but disaster.

To have been female and read
who but duras:
panther breathing hot on the neck.
What is at risk?

My doubt is my wager every time,

and every time I look at the sea
to see that many plates
sliding from that many cabinets
drunk as wood. I know that's where you live and still

the rug pulled out from under you, you
lie on the floor

pitch from an eastern white pine
cone all closed up, guzzling down.

What is to be done but tax, regulate
rebel, arm and fire.

Talking into a drum I became
suspicious about my motivations.

No, is that an ethics.

To carry a vocabulary, marysia:
what is this kind of intelligence
it is terrifying.

I go home from the
restaurant take the
title of her poem slap
it around some. Being a
poet is being nonchalant in
restaurants, saying not to then
taking off your clothes in a
restaurant. That sleeve we
share in the collective sweater
getting sopping wet. Everybody
has an emergency. Everybody
has a vocabulary. I cut my hair
you end up plucking a sleeve.

Dear marysia.
Today I want to cry. Today I still
don't know what goes on when we watch
dance. Nothing is going to mean
what it does because this is the body.
There is no qualitative difference between doing
an action and not doing an action (both have
consequences). I still don't know what kind
of talking is helpful or unhelpful. We show up
by different doors wearing the same sweater, we leave
by different doors also, somebody asks a question

somebody comes to sit by me, somebody mentions that
two half presences sharing a presence might only
be an accidental value of the work, we have these
proclivities, kristel offers me a pair of scissors, our emergencies
converge. Is my not knowing today any different from
yesterday or last year or ten years. I don't
actually care about the nobody at the end of writing
marysia but the somebody and the
somebody and the somebody else who engendered
it. To be near. It's not 'healing.'

But other ways to be embroiled in the social.
But other ways to be embroiled in the social.
Is that always about power.

These are gifts.
Some resonate
Some don't:
    break off a piece from your mouth
    this gesture entirely personal, but not yet my own
    (these are gifts).
Who is this gift for.

::

"I don't have control over my questions now."

all the girls in the restaurants
nonchalance is feigned always
like rittenhouse in february
not walking into anthropologie
not doing a thing (you show me
again and again) has just as many
qualitative consequences as doing
a thing. you say this shit has consequences
I say "browse" you say
"perceive" as in unloose
as in gate or doorway –

shot silk mustard glimpse:
you cite my body
I cite your question
say, "no permission without persimmons"
you say, "I've been thinking about
cadence and the symbolic order..."
why don't you call me
what we both know I am

   "...inside philadelphia, inside the northeast, inside the galaxy, inside
the universe, but first inside the mother..."?

first, not to know – then an us?
don't know how to do this with my body
don't know how to not do this with my body.
meg will ask annie about objects
meg will say why do you draw a line there.
no I don't have control
over my questions, now

::

What is it to write beside

to let go of the anxiety of influence
to let go of the anxiety of order.

you don't remember
the things you say
because you feel them.
because you feel them
a month later, I tell my grandmother
about the plastic bags, the
balaclava. one year since she lost
hans, thirty years ago she sent
him home, someone pissed on the
lawn, dresden, his sons waited.

when you're waiting, the rules
change. your clothes, for instance, or
a name. it's only driving back
on the new jersey turnpike
it hits me: she laughed and said,
"you have a sense of humor, girl"
she said, "it's good to have all kinds
of friends" and told me about a friend
in fact, a woman. we want to sing
the manifesto about the slipperiness of
language but the problem is that all
the words we shared, written or spoke

none of them did go away, but have only
gathered us in.

and the balaclava, the
plastic bags. since one is not
one, is at risk already.

having this sense of humor
that takes place so regularly and
satisfyingly on the axis of selection.
gags on the level of the signifiers.
the replacements standing in for:
    ask me for a clothing gesture,
    show up with bags of clothes.

if the problem you are currently having
in your art practice that needs me most
were a government funded research station
on a remote island
and it were talking to another research
station in a different country
far away, what is the most beautiful thing
one could say to another
in their shared language?

yes, I too am here. I too am
listen

::

Having
exhausted the
possibilities

  for green

war
photography and scale

 population by
disease   blue

 spread the
denser

if
you humor   me
predisposed

to alter if

I humor   you
to wonder

  that
black sun

::

I will misunderstand for a long time
"the costumes make me really mad"
"pissed off about not doing the practice"
a pushing, a pushing away from
your very nauseous intercostals
hook and sink her.
in the wake of *failure's queerest passion*
nonchalance is a sinking ship
and you want words that are social for our movement
(the pleasure of love):

well, this text is a body too
don't say, your work makes me sick
say, your work gives me a physical sensation
I associate with nausea.
the way we can put
a magician inside the dance and a
book in a book
compliment a sweater then
slide hood over face...
how does writing become a poem but
disaster and a failed sea map.
and if failure is when a process ends
and we are left wanting more?

I want to give up this
poor definition of feminism as
approximate nausea.

::

Now tell me
tell only me and three others:
do you ever mourn
your own thoughts?

that whole year I stole
your orchids over and over.
didn't mean to they just
slid out on the studio floor.
like something we can do
eleven times and the twelfth time
it really will be a repetition.

property that is participation.

dear meg. to get to "we" *I*
might have to stop wanting it so bad.
this mad longing is singing to whatever's unloosed as in
to see the ship we need
the discourse that could be as fog
and equally much the constellated
nonsense trope of the yellow moon
and also and also.
why do people collect things?
a jury box would lead me straight to you
just like a bruise in the game it's
just like me to lose.

you and I, were we born into her wreck
so seeing it is backwards.
sure I'd like to geometrically constellate
damaged material, but can't seem to stop
picking up and putting down this mug.
it says 'I heart verisimilitude.'
or maybe 'I learned to heart verisimilitude
at eighteen in connecticut, can't stop now.'

somebody's mad when you bring your own coffee.
somebody's worried about words how they don't
go away, everything stays as sound wave
but actions too, right? perceptions too?
that's where everything gets gummy, since what we don't
perceive is also the result of frameworks
sometimes helpful or absurd.

I'll pay you a visit, leave my cards
smattered on that lawn and go home
that's a poem. no, we're doing it anyway
even though we're not so compatible – that's
a poem. *all those interior cavities*
brimming with disagreements, too much
time instead of not enough. *come live with*
me then, 'cuz there's nothing that's not it –

I said, "sail from all boats!" every day
an oar, now tell me...

what is the gesture that's female and
funny like the panther duras?
how fall in
love with a singular fact
before what we know?
I want to know it but one day soon I'm
going to want to lick something
more. salty and blubbery and interior.
come and live
where we can plant
each other's money like acorns
and every diaphragm
unpeels an unexpected
swath:
the morning glory
so seedy, so
ancient *on the gate.*

under that canopy, your most dreaded
question many others
entirely different occasion
to ask another tree—

if you sing me there
your most authentic melodrama
might actually get to

        share it :: dread it

and I promise not to
leave you any
  more

::

but but my heart
is a
trickster
too:

"letter
from my body
to your body":
what is the
sensation
of being read
of reading the
sensation of
embodied
critique:

in this narrow band
of infinity, not
everything is
available

"all kinds of weird
reasons" she said
"why people
have to go
about learning
to do perfectly
ordinary things":

but but:
doing
this thing or that
thing or not that
thing or this

thing isn't
an action:

is I want
to take you
where we
are already
shine:

how long
without making
a choice:
this long:
this
winter-long
this: what does
that this say
about the
other this

these narrows
sensation:

and if
our 'art practice'

were a research
station living:
thistles:

what else
could it long
for but measure and
time: more time than
measure:

this much in luck:
this much in discretion:

(to look upon
the sea and see
oneself: the kind
of person we

all wanted never
to become is to
come up by the
sea) a kind of wailing
a kind of crooning
that kind of jig:

(thistle ethics)

just don't call me
don't call me
don't you call me
what we both know
I am

:a seismograph
:a sail out of
:flavor and season

:a map that never
stops

                              :to loose

but we sooooo flap

::

Water directed
to where
it's going will find

a source.
the all inclusive
fact

our facile bodies
so facile with havoc
on a mean.

you feel out of
scale, this binky
the love object
fake blood
stage death
all the king's men
all the king's chairs
on top of all those pages
in beauchamp-feuillet.

to unevent the dance
he says, "that's not
culture, but my first
book was about it."

buckets dip, on a mean.

we're going to make
cookies with our possible futures
insert little messages.
we'll carry them in a plastic
sack on the plane, and like
st. augustine instead of eating
our own words,
break off a piece from your mouth

(did you open)

::

Your beautiful rage
at aboutness
is neither beautiful nor
your own

my body made up
of places and times
other people haven't
been too

helios dips
finger in paternal
soup, spreads
d.n.a. on every
page the top of
sat the king or totalizing
I know resist but presence
or that which demands

your beautiful
aboutness

::

Not only
the symbols we
shared but their
combinations, rotations
not up to the
task to hold a
float a world long
sunk or lost.
no boats
no loss.
like water
could be
some kind of
feminine
humor, not pinning
grove just gags
to stand the time
at the level of
those willowy
replacements.
like water
could stand
with anything but
whosoever's performance
emergency still
what how floats

:: move the rock
not the balloon

::

Hair

a problem
I am
having: *what if*
every cell
in my
body let's
consider
solved already
meg I have a
point I'm not just
asking what if
questions.
what if every
cell were a
seismograph
on a government
funded research
station on a
remote island
set to constantly
register the
following
concession: I may
prefer
you in the
plural

but that's
just the jig
how we
know things
feel things
are. what if
while you
read this
tonight
every cell
in my/your body
were a constantly

falling asleep
prickle constantly
in the darkness just
eating
talking
failing
dial perfectly
set to register
our eating, not eating
our research
just the fact of
you, just
like that
stepping
out for
some air?

in a three
part leap

the second part
is 'in the
air.'

for fun
we try
to scale it:

~~my doubt is my wager.~~
my doubt is my favor.

::

::

(Okay
I can't tell
you what is
political about my
poem writing
body the living
I have
to be doing to
write the
poems *I can*
tell you
what is political
about where
a poem *starts*
and when
and next
to who)

::

Having
exhausted the possibilities
for green
we turned to null island:

a trouble-shooting country
of indeterminate sovereignty class
located at the zero, zero
formatted to keep errant
coordinates away from your map

a detailed and undulating
forest from above

no you can't
have a personal
symbology
but you can have a fashionable
desire for the quake

to lay one's body at the fault
its eventual rumble.

your scale can even be bad
on purpose, fashionably late
hans, waiting for his sister
to finish on that lawn
exhausting nothing
not the parsing of distinction
nor its lack.

went looking for
the burned out rainforest, turns out
the enabling structure
has its own politics:
even control-burned trees grow back so fast
we need the exact date and time to place your order
...and so, deprived of black, I returned to green

this is the memorial
this is the fire

who are you without our references
but anyone else—

just another blue-faced doll
in a sweater chosen for you
by the people in this room.

and if to symbol were a process
we could share
not before, nor
after but as
it takes place?

"it was social when you said
come with you
into the green space.

"brought every green
thing in your apartment
into the basement, tied our
heads together, played the
viewfinder game.

"it felt so wrong"
you say, "having our
heads tied together."

null island
slips us the eventual finger
and in its wake
I humor you:
    a donut
    a meter in diameter
    or square
what is our shape?

don't pretend you didn't
lie awake nights, too
crying just a little
cause there's a million better bands
when they told you about the zero
singers who can drum
figuring its weight
and in its wake
to wonder

that black sun

::

When pressed for water
hard-pressed to answer
going down to view the wreck
going up to dia beacon to view the
shrink-wrapped car parts—
who gets the gags on the signifiers
like they do, reflects them like they do.
the time you poured into me
was a serious thing
your presence was a
velvet substitution.
oh you made a mean topos
when I didn't know how to not become
you know, some territory—
people can come, graze
take a little thirst from each rubber
house plant practice
fortunes in each other's
dictionaries except
my house
has a faucet
running

::

things that take
the time they
take:
eating
talking.
do you know
how to
make a move
that's not
gestural.
things that
take
to answer
your gift
I had to learn
about time and
vision, the difference
I made a child's
garden into which
all experience
could pour.
I made a
fountain.
I made a
signifying
function. someone

said let's
do clothing gestures
every day, and I
showed up at the
house with bags
and bags
of clothes.
we're on
a bus.
headphones.
sleepers.
it's a quiet
thing in the
center of someone's
abdomen
to lean to
waiver. we
are on the
same bus.
I said gestural
joke, meant
to point towards
time and
multiple
contradictory
frameworks.
read kenward
elmslie's
moving right along
because I'm
leaving the city

in which you
live, find it
at a bookshop
along route
send you a photo
of the cover
along with my
cat. I want to give
up this poor
definition
of feminism, too.
and the wild
ponies? want
to take you somewhere
you can see and hear
and say the kinds
of things only
there. where?
oh, assateague in the
off seas, only
two of us in this
motel. but meg
you knew already
it's a bell
twinkling inside
your question. I want
to take you
somewhere so
specific it doesn't
matter where we
go. no gesture

is a decision before
what we share
hunts us, too.
time is a lonely.
straight through the news.
straight there the heart.

gifts

11:
A tracking shot is a moral act.
—Jean-Luc Godard

The Rug Pulled Out From Underneath You, You Lie on the Floor.
—Gallery show, Hedreen Gallery, Seattle University. Winter 2013. Dawn Cerny &
Shaw Osha, curators.

13:
I met a poet, she said she didn't like the smell of it / then took her clothes off in a
restaurant for the hell of it...
—The Presidents of the United States of America, "Naked and Famous"

14:
...of course, maniacal bouts of writing, learning to address no one...
—Maggie Nelson, *The Argonauts*

My gesture's not my own.
—Rosemarie Waldrop, "Three pieces"

15:
All the girls in the restaurants / pretending to be so nonchalant...
—Patty Griffin, "Be Careful"

Why don't you call me what we both know I am?
—James Blake, "Why Don't You Call Me"

21:
...a kind of queer optimism born equally from the passion of failure and the
pleasure of love.
—Rob Halpern, "Rethood Onroda's 'Conceptual Writing,' An Essay By Rob Halpern"

"Don't say, your work makes me sick. Say, your work gives me a physical sensation I associate with nausea."
—Sadie Benning, in conversation with the author

22:
...just like me / you were one big bruise / in the game of life we were playing to lose...
—The Magnetic Fields, "Two Characters In Search of a Country Song"

23:
I came to explore the wreck / Words are maps.
—Adrienne Rich, "Diving Into the Wreck"

Come live with me...Our interior cavities / Brimming with / Disagreeable substances.
—John Yau, "Ill-advised Love Poem"

24:
"What is a gesture that is funny and female and sexy all at once?"
—Emmanuelle Deplech-Ramey & Charlotte Ford, Clown Striptease workshop, Headlong Dance Camp, 2008

If I could still extrapolate / the morning-glory on the gate / from St. Petersburg in history—but it's too late
—Adrienne Rich, "From Morning-Glory to Petersburg"

26:
"In this narrow band of infinity, not everything is available."
—Jumatatu Poe, The Switching workshop, The Mascher Space Cooperative, Winter, 2016

34:
"I know resist, but presence or that which demands it?"
—Gregory Holt, studio practice, Susan Rethorst's studio, Winter, 2015

35:

Politicians are like a balloon tied to a rock. If we swat at them, they may sway to the left or the right. But, tied down, they can only go so far. Instead of batting at them, we should move the rock: people's activated social values.

—Daniel Hunter, *Strategy and Soul*

36:

"What if every cell in my body..."
—Deborah Hay, choreography

I prefer 'you' in the plural.
 —John Ashbery, "A Blessing in Disguise"

37:

"The second part of a three-part leap is in the air."
—Kathryn TeBordo, choreography, Workshop for Potential Movement, 2008

40:

Text in this poem inspired by a Q&A with Jonathan Burrows after he and Matteo Fargion peformed "Facing Front" at The Neighborhood House Theater, Philadelphia, June 2015.

41:

A trouble-shooting country of indeterminate sovereignty class...a detailed and undulating forest from above...and so, deprived of black, I returned to green.
—Laura Kurgan, *Close Up At A Distance: Mapping, Technology and Politics*

..imagine what it might mean to lay one's body down at the fault – the body as seismograph, registering the crisis.
—Rob Halpern, "Committing the Fault: Notes Towards a Faulty Narrative Practice"

42:

"Is dance the memorial or the fire?"
—Gregory Holt, correspondence, 2011

That blue represents millions of dollars and countless jobs and it's sort of comical how you think that you've made a choice that exempts you from the fashion industry when in fact you're wearing a sweater that was selected for you by the people in this room.
—Lauren Weisberger, *The Devil Wears Prada*

44:

We're not gonna make it! / Cause there's a million better bands / Singers who can drum...
—The Presidents of the United States of America, "We're Not Gonna Make It"

46:

"Can you make a movement decision that is not gestural?"
—Meg Foley, Meaning is a Muscle workshop, Headlong Dance Camp, 2008

::

processes

risk :: nonchalance was written alongside two dance processes.

action is primary is a choreographic task, a score for solo and group improvisation, as well as the name of a dance production that premiered at the Icebox Project Space at Crane Arts in Philadelphia during the Spring of 2016, choreographed and developed by Meg Foley.

As Meg describes it, "the central task of *action is primary* is 'holding what you are doing at the center of what you are doing, even as it moves towards new centers.'"

The score is practiced in the studio but not necessarily performed in the following order: do what you need; action is primary; single focus, multiple body; intervention; authentic melodrama; visualization; talking; all five at once; action is primary; residue. For the Icebox production, Meg asked me and several other writers and artists to make a response to *aip* from within our own media.

To prepare to write *risk :: nonchalance*, I visited rehearsals periodically, over the course of several months. I also took a workshop to learn the score, and practiced on my own. Mostly, I witnessed.

Armed with a notepad or computer, I hovered around the edges, watching the four performers work, argue and explore. After only a few visits, I couldn't help but notice that my presence – and indeed, the presence of any of us watching, because there were periodic visitors, improvisation experts and dramaturges and funders and people asked to provide an "outside eye" – had some effect, however small and inextricable and impossible-to-pin-down effect, on the action.

An itch. A tickle. A familiar discomfort. That peculiar sensation that indicates one's presence is neither immune nor un-implicated, that the audience is here: We were watching, wearing matching sweaters, and we were – in a way that was hard to define at the time, and remains hard, in writing, to make tangible – nonetheless, at least partially, responsible.

aip is articulated in terms of actions. Again and again, I watched performers push their capacities for action to the brink, performing the score. I don't know if the performers would say they did this; that is what I saw.

A movement, shape or relationship can be an action – so can their lack or obverse, the way around or through. Meg writes:

> I chose the word action in an effort to look at the physical identity and experience of things like remembering or looking that in first glance don't have a movement signifier. So it can be a broad frame that includes the constellation or network of an activity (which may involve movement, space, time, relationship, etc.)...

I began thinking about Bojana Cvejić's discussion of an action as a primary material unit of social choreography.[1] What I saw being choreographed in *aip*: a way in which the social takes place.

In a town like Philadelphia, where dancers live in intertwined communities, and expect to work with one another in ever-rotating configurations, this means that the choreography itself overspills any one performance or production.

If the choreography overspills, and is care – is one way performers care for one another.

Meg takes issue with my observation that *aip* asks performers and audience to identify and redefine what an action is. She writes:

> I resist the word "identifying" because to me it communicates naming, which isn't necessary in *aip*, although not out of the question, and to me it suggests an objective selection process.
>
> The latter can certainly occur, but I always situate that experience as an action in and of itself – to decide to move away from yourself/where you are or to select a particularity about what you're doing – the first action is the decisive impulse and/or objectivity.
>
> So your attention is not so much "on identifying an action" as it is actively, simultaneously tracing and filling, recognizing your attention and its temporal shifts as structural to the activity you are doing. They are not separate, and that attention itself is an action.

From this perspective, *action is primary* is a process that gets at questions of reciprocity, attending, recognizing, acting in that.

If, irregardless "this shit has consequences."

If those consequences form in continual relation to our unfolding attention as it fills the shapes to which we blend.

If this process gets at questions of agency – questions that are central to performing life – questions that are central to radical queer life, also.

Meanwhile:

I found myself amidst a messy, meandering, and personal interdisciplinary studio exchange with a dancer and friend. We began by deliberately not collaborating. Instead we traded questions from our individual projects, and searched for movement and writing processes we could do together, to respond. We worked toward a state we called embodied criticality, and which we stole.[2] We worked in chunks of self-made residencies for a year or so before deciding to collaborate, then made a dance that was a relationship that was a dance, which we took to Toronto to perform at a series called *Flow Chart*, armed with 300 custom-made fortune cookies and some posters of individual poems from *risk :: nonchalance*.

What is a poem besides disaster?

When we began, I had questions about repetition and reference and line break, because I didn't use any of them in my first book, and I brought these to the studio. In *A Choreographic Mind*, Rethorst points to the joke at the center of so many dances: *We know so well that nothing is the same as anything else that we laugh to hear or say it, but in dance making we often proceed as if one thing were in fact another, as if the reality of people moving in one way or another is the same as our idea (either preceding or following) of it.*[3] We traded seismographs. We forgot it was a process in which we were going to forget everything we knew.

Yet the movement is not the same as the words we use to describe it. All those decisions we think come before as after the sentence that made us over into someone who could do that, who could say *I do this, I do that.*[4]

Repetition, reference, line-break: so of course, disaster.

Or, perhaps that brought me to the studio in the first place: one email said, "Come tear a hole in my book!" before I'd written it.

During our dress rehearsal, my friend says, "if you're faced with a false binary, raise both poles!" We are having a fight about what belongs inside and outside and I'm not sure why, but this fight is generative.

Shrugging, trace each gesture back and forth across that ribboning trajectory; it's the wobble that accounts for the wager.

I say, "I want us to take our movement out of all the frameworks in which it is normally read, and to expose those frameworks, what is messed up about them. So the movement can be just what it is."

But tell me, who wants to read a primer on how to drink a glass of water kinetically vs. kinesthetically while standing in the multiple contested seas?[5]

I thought that maybe if I crafted the experience before writing – if that were crafted too – that illusive, ever-problematic *experience* that is supposed to move us, inspire the poem – maybe crafting that together would get us out of certain problems. And instead?

> Caught in what you call *your beautiful rage at aboutness* I can only perform the gags at the level of the signifiers.

> You ask how we get to meaning, if it's ice cream and sorbet, or ice cream or sorbet, or possibilities you can't yet imagine.

> I ask you to rub ice cream and sorbet on my face while I tell you about my rage at aboutness.

You decline in some confusion, then proceed to eat a bowl of ice cream from my freezer, very fast.

I slowly erase all syntax implying cause and effect from this description of our process – a quiet performance stolen from language poetry, a gesture with which you may or may not be familiar.

I worry about the ethics of sharing a practice without sharing references.

I had a problem of context, processes that wouldn't stay put, that poured through. Water's not a pinning grove, I know. One score says ask for help, so I am asking you (in the plural): *I'm writing in case anyone can recommend writing or art projects that address an ethical dilemma to do with how writing moves from within one process or community to another, and how 'producers' make decisions around navigating those borders.* Processes are separate, but take place in parallel (is this body a vessel)?

At customs, we smuggle in the cookies: I am asked more questions, because I am more honest but you are more trustworthy. Or is it the other way around? Does it anger you that I can't remember which we decided? Because I know now what you meant when you said you wanted words that are social to describe our movement, and this is social:

how we mistake, again and again, affect for intent,[6] in exchange for the language of sincerity.

So you can say, "thank you for taking these crazy risks with me" and I can say, "but I am not really risking anything, be

cause our whole agreement is that we will take these crazy
risks with one another" and somebody can think, *yeah, right.*

What reference does between bodies, media? Combine it with line
breaks, and repetition, and it starts to look a lot like—but of course,
like love:

> *I'm so vain*
> *You bet*
> *I think this*
> *song is*
> *about me. Don't*
> *I? Don't I?*
> *Don't I?*[7]

When I humor you, when you humor me: can't seem to stop picking
up and putting down this mug. Some pretty toxic signs and symbols
rearrange time and relation into a fairly tolerable read. Processes are
particular but overlapping contradictions (persons, labors, relations,
networks of cells, networks of needing, questioning, seeing, not
seeing, the sensation of critique). Threading, sorting, I can no longer tell
which process spawned what goose chase, and whose goose
engendered my showing up for the hunt. I write, because this appears
to be a writing action:

(Whatever is outside you singing already your outside self).

But page or song? I write: *If you can think of any art projects or research that
deal with this dilemma, please send.*

Like body practices, or any relation that relies on scale, takes time
and living through the materials, like all the questions we donned

renaissance man body style to repeat with a difference,[8] reference won't stay put. It's a jiggle. It's a jiggling. It's a slopping and a pouring. It's a disappearing noun. It's a self-replicating gag. It's pay it forward. It's the rug pulled out and it's the sinking ship and it's the queer love of failure and it holds water, weight and time that's up and then, no longer in control of my questions, I have to ask: Who else stands here with me, all up to our calves? Who else, contested, leaks – whose wobble wages?

Maybe it is not possible to explain the stakes, maybe it is only possible to explain the how, the process. I want poems to be this how, this process. I want to fail poems in this way.

What is the difference between shake, shimmer and shine?[9] Years later, in the poem, maybe we are.

[1] Bojana Cvejić, *Public Sphere by Performance*

[2] A source text for this collaboration was Irit Rogoff, *Smuggling: An Embodied Criticality*

[3] Susan Rethorst, *A Choreographic Mind*

[4] Frank O'Hara, on the subject of what is a *Frank O'Hara poem*

[5] A book I found in the Temple library dance collection and have since lost track of includes instructions on how to drink a glass of water kinetically vs. kinesthetically.

[6] Susan Rethorst, *A Choreographic Mind*: "'But it's supposed to be about...' the oft heard lament, the mistaking of intention for affect."

[7] Carly Simon, *You're So Vain*, lyrics (pronouns switched)

[8] In *Volition* (published by Printed Matter), Gregg Bordowitz makes a book entirely out of questions.
While living across the country from my friend, I proposed that we read this book together; later, our choreographic score consisted of writing and responding to questions, as a practice and live performance.

[9] Choreography, Kathryn TeBordo, The Workshop for Potential Movement

acknowledgments

risk :: nonchalance came into being by invitation: early drafts of the poems were commissioned for Meg Foley's production of *Action Is Primary* at the Icebox Project Space at Crane Arts, Philadelphia (April 2016). My special thanks and gratitude are due to Meg and to the performers for allowing me to witness your work: Kristel Baldoz, Annie Wilson and Marysia Stokłosa, and to the production team, especially Thomas Choinacky and Marissa Perel. Innumerable thanks are also due to Gregory Holt, for the year-ish of shared studio practice, and for the particular dance informing these poems: for your questions! To Susan Rethorst and Amelia Earhart for material support for that practice. To more dance makers than I can name here: for conversation, workshop, your questions.

My deepest, sincere gratitude to Sharon, Gillian, Ken, Rusty, and everyone at Omnidawn for your care with this collection, and to Hoa Nguyen. A huge thank you to Emily Abendroth for shrewd acts of reading, and to Evan McGonagill, Rusty Morrison, Christina Gesualdi, Aimee Harrison, Gregory Laynor, Joshua Beckman, and Beau Martin for generous comments on the closing essay. Thank you to Emmy Bright for the cover art! To Jeremy Hoovenar for inviting me to perform at the Zinc Bar Sunday Series. To my parents and the Middle Bits singers for your support. Finally: fireworks of thanks to Eero Hagen, for illustrating these during *A.I.P.*, and for stupefying acts of vision and care – inside and out.

Photo by Eero Hagen

laura neuman lives in Philadelphia and is the author of one previous book, *Stop the Ocean* (Stockport Flats) and one chapbook, *The Busy Life* (Gazing Grain). Her/their poems have appeared in *Troubling the Line: Trans and Genderqueer Poetry and Poetics* (Nightboat and Chax), *The Brooklyn Rail*, *The Encyclopedia Project*, *Fact-simile*, *small portions*, *X-Poetics*, *EOAGH*, and her/their writing has been supported by The Fund for Poetry.

risk :: nonchalance
by laura neuman

Cover image: *The Repressed / The Return of the Repressed* by Emmy Bright,
silkscreen and marker on paper.

Text set in Century Gothic and Garamond 3 LT Std

Cover and interior design by Sharon Zetter

Offset printed in the United States
by Edwards Brothers Malloy, Ann Arbor, Michigan
On 55# Glatfelter B18 Antique
Acid Free Archival Quality Recycled Paper

Publication of this book was made possible in part by gifts from:
The Clorox Company
The New Place Fund
Robin & Curt Caton

Omnidawn Publishing
Oakland, California
2017

Rusty Morrison & Ken Keegan, senior editors & co-publishers
Gillian Olivia Blythe Hamel, managing editor
Cassandra Smith, poetry editor & book designer
Sharon Zetter, poetry editor, book designer & development officer
Avren Keating, poetry editor, fiction editor & marketing assistant
Liza Flum, poetry editor
Juliana Paslay, fiction editor
Gail Aronson, fiction editor
Trisha Peck, marketing assistant
Cameron Stuart, marketing assistant
Natalia Cinco, marketing assistant
Maria Kosiyanenko, marketing assistant
Emma Thomason, administrative assistant
SD Sumner, copyeditor
Kevin Peters, *OmniVerse* Lit Scene editor
Sara Burant, *OmniVerse* reviews editor